# Alan Bullard

# Psalmi Penitentiales

A Lenten sequence based on the Penitential Psalms and Ubi caritas

for SATB and organ or piano

MUSIC DEPARTMENT

OXFORD
UNIVERSITY PRESS

# Contents

# Composer's note

*Psalmi Penitentiales* (Penitential Psalms) consists of three main movements which comprise extracts, in Latin, from psalms particularly associated with the season of Lent. Each of these movements includes musical material derived from the plainchant antiphon for Maundy Thursday, 'Ubi caritas', and arrangements of this antiphon are also interspersed between the psalms as four short movements, forming a prelude, two interludes, and a postlude. The accompaniment, originally written for organ, may be played on the piano by making some adjustments: pianists may spread chords, omit small notes if necessary, take some LH notes in the RH, and double the organ pedal line an octave lower where feasible. In order to give the work added flexibility in performance, the psalms may also be performed separately.

Duration: *c.*18 minutes.

## OXFORD
### UNIVERSITY PRESS

Great Clarendon Street, Oxford OX2 6DP, United Kingdom

Oxford is a registered trade mark of Oxford University Press
in the UK and in certain other countries

© Oxford University Press 2017

Alan Bullard has asserted his right under the Copyright, Designs
and Patents Act, 1988, to be identified as the Composer of this Work

Database right Oxford University Press (maker)

First published 2017

Impression: 1

ISBN 978–0–19–351900–8

Printed in Great Britain on acid-free paper by
Halstan & Co. Ltd, Amersham, Bucks.

*Commissioned by the Waltham Singers, director Andrew Fardell, with a generous bequest from Peter Andrews*

# Psalmi Penitentiales

## A Lenten sequence based on the Penitential Psalms and Ubi caritas

**ALAN BULLARD**

## 1. Antiphon: Ubi caritas (i)

Antiphon for Maundy Thursday
arr. ALAN BULLARD

[1] Where charity and love are, God is there. [2] Christ's love has gathered us into one.

* Solo soprano/alto could be offstage

First performed by the Waltham Singers, directed by Andrew Fardell, with Laurence Lyndon-Jones (organ), at King Edward VI Grammar School, Chelmsford, on 18 March 2017.

4

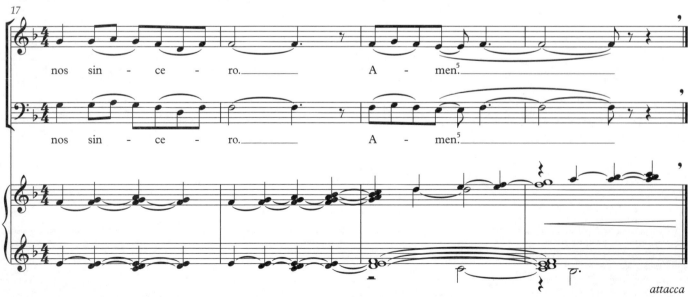

*attacca*

[3] Let us rejoice and be pleased in him. [4] Let us fear, and let us love the living God. [5] And may we love each other with a sincere heart. Amen.

# 2. Domine, ne in furore tuo arguas me

Psalm 6: 1–9

ALAN BULLARD

[1] O Lord, rebuke me not in thine anger,

[2]neither chasten me in thy hot displeasure.  [3]Have mercy upon me, O Lord; for I am weak:  [4]O Lord, heal me; for my bones are vexed.

optional SOLO or SEMI-CHORUS
*p* espress.

optional SOLO or SEMI-CHORUS
*p* espress.

optional SOLO or SEMI-CHORUS
*p* espress.

[10]in the grave who shall give thee thanks?   [11]I am weary with my groaning;   [12]all the night make I my bed to swim;

<sup></sup>13 I water my couch with my tears. 14 Mine eye is consumed because of grief; 15 it waxeth old because of all mine enemies.

[16]Depart from me, all ye workers of iniquity;

[17]for the Lord hath heard the voice of my weeping. [18] The Lord hath heard my supplication;

# 3. Antiphon: Ubi caritas (ii)

Antiphon for Maundy Thursday
arr. ALAN BULLARD

[1] Where charity and love are, God is there. [2] As we are gathered into one body, [3] Beware, lest we be divided in mind.
[4] Let evil impulses stop, let controversy cease, [5] And may Christ our God be in our midst. Amen.

# 4. De profundis

Psalm 129 (130)

ALAN BULLARD

[1] Out of the depths have I cried unto thee.

² Lord, hear my voice:

[3] let thine ears be attentive to the voice of my supplications.   [4] If thou, Lord, shouldest mark iniquities, O Lord, who shall stand?

[5]But there is forgiveness with thee, that thou mayest be feared, O Lord.

[6] I wait for the Lord, my soul doth wait, and in his word do I hope. [7] My soul waiteth for the Lord more than they that watch for the morning.
[8] Let Israel hope in the Lord:

⁹for with the Lord there is mercy, ¹⁰and with him is plenteous redemption.

[11] And he shall redeem Israel from all his iniquities.

*attacca*

# 5. Antiphon: Ubi caritas (iii)

Antiphon for Maundy Thursday
arr. ALAN BULLARD

[1] Where charity and love are, God is there.   [2] And may we with the saints also,   [3] See thy face in glory, O Christ our God:
[4] The joy that is immense and good,   [5] Unto the ages through infinite ages. Amen.

# 6. Domine, exaudi orationem meam

Psalm 101(102): 1–2, 11–12

ALAN BULLARD

<sup>2</sup>and let my cry come unto thee.

[5] in the day when I call answer me speedily.

# 7. Antiphon: Ubi caritas (iv)

Antiphon for Maundy Thursday
arr. ALAN BULLARD

[1] Where charity and love are, God is there.  [2] Christ's love has gathered us into one.  [3] Let us rejoice and be pleased in him.

*Solo soprano/alto could be offstage
†Piano: repeat LH notes as appropriate

*October 2016*

[4]Let us fear, and let us love the living God.　[5]And may we love each other with a sincere heart. Amen.